每年的一月一日是新年。

新年也叫"元旦"。"元旦"是开始的意思,就是新年的第一天。

很多国家都会庆祝元旦。

很多国家在元旦这一天放假。

有的人和家人一起庆祝元旦。

有的人和朋友一起庆祝元旦。

人们都希望新的一年有新的开始。

人们都希望新的一年顺顺利利、健健康康。

Glossary

	Pinyin	English Definition
新年	xīn nián	New Year
元旦	yuán dàn	New Year's Day
开始	kāi shǐ	beginning
意思	yì si	meaning
国家	guó jiā	country
庆祝	qìng zhù	to celebrate
放假	fàng jià	to have a holiday
希望	xī wàng	to hope
顺顺利利	shùn shùn lì lì	smooth
健健康康	jiàn jiàn kāng kāng	healthy

Copyright © 2022 by Level Learning INC.

All rights reserved. No part of this book in whole or part may be reproduced without written permission from the publisher

Author: Jingyao Qi, Level Learning

Simplified Chinese Edition

- This is the last page of this book. -

www.ingramcontent.com/pod-product-compliance
Lightning Source LLC
Chambersburg PA
CBHW041217070526
44583CB00001B/19